EDWARD GOREY

The Water Flowers

Congdon & Weed, Inc.
NEW YORK

Copyright © 1982 by Edward Gorey
Distributor's ISBN: 0-312-92928-5
Publisher's ISBN: 0-86553-059-9
Library of Congress Catalog Card Number: 82-73193
Published by Congdon & Weed, Inc.
298 Fifth Avenue, New York, N.Y. 10001
Distributed by St. Martin's Press
175 Fifth Avenue, New York, N.Y. 10010
Printed in the United States of America
First Edition

For Isobel Grassie

It began snowing early in the afternoon.

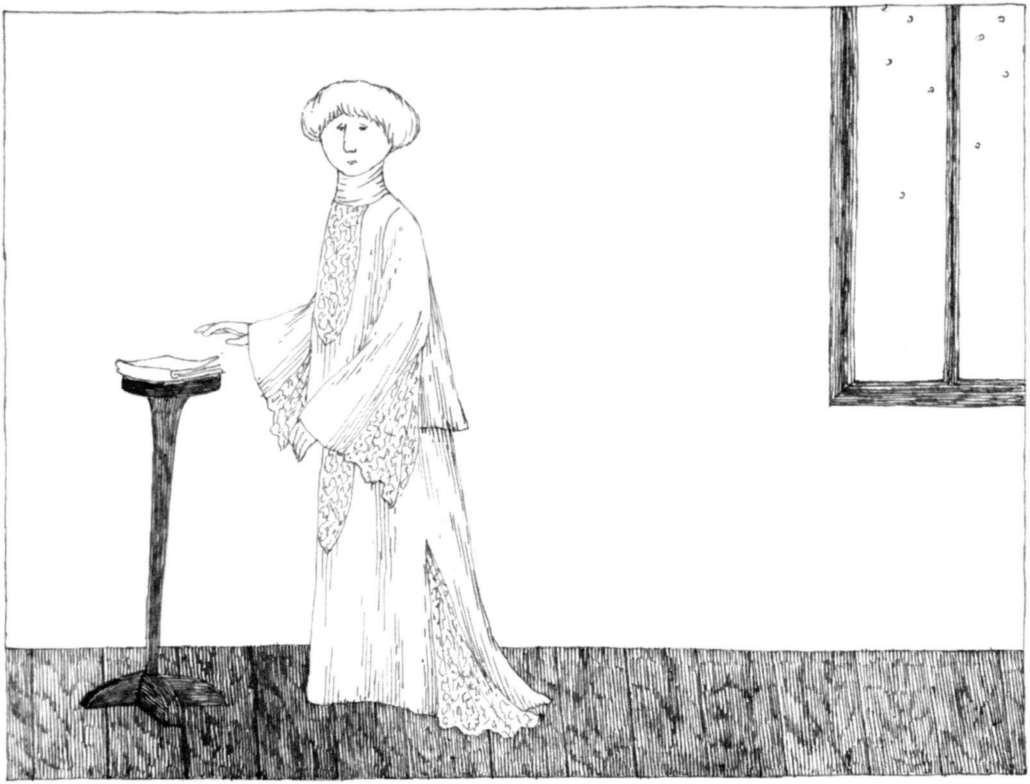

Jane settled herself on the sofa with a novelette in a yellow paper cover.

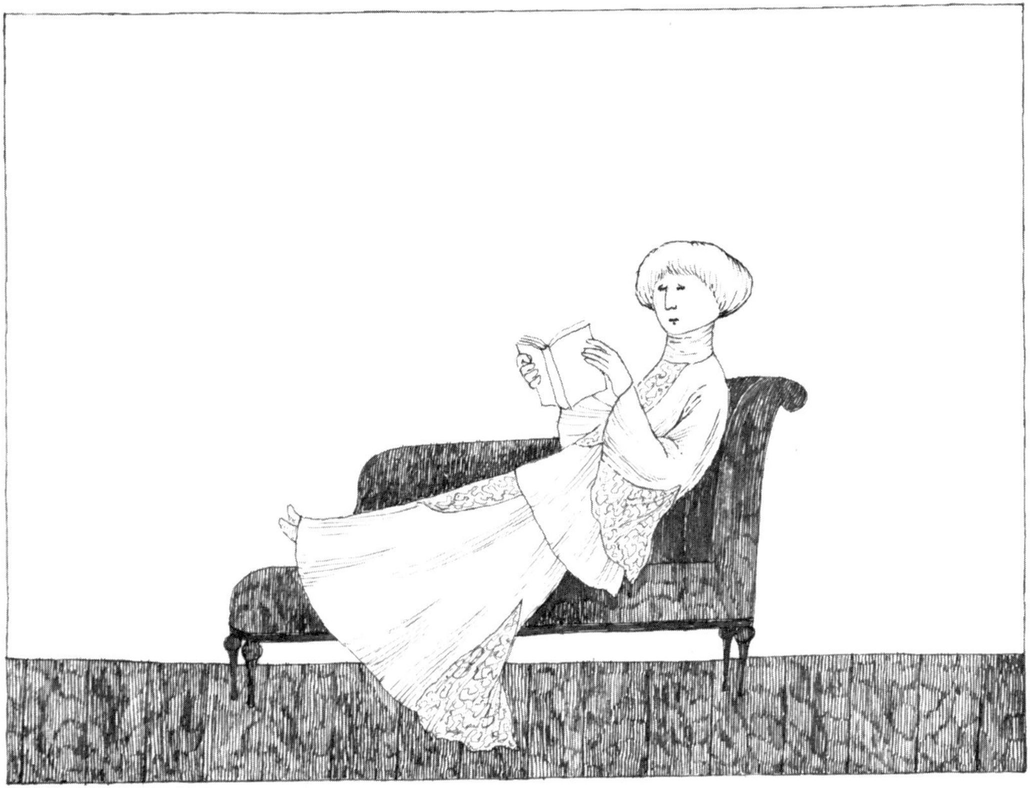

The wind rose and the snow came down harder.

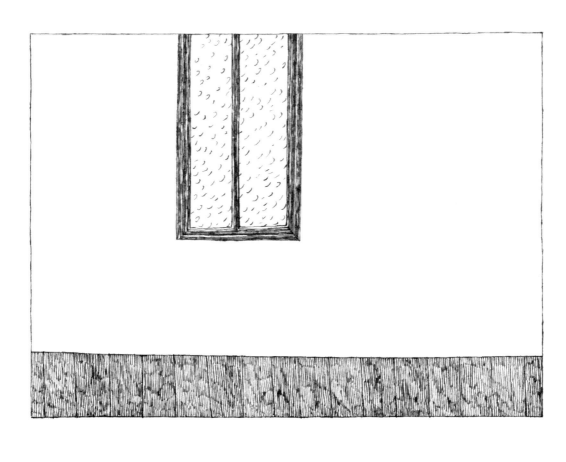

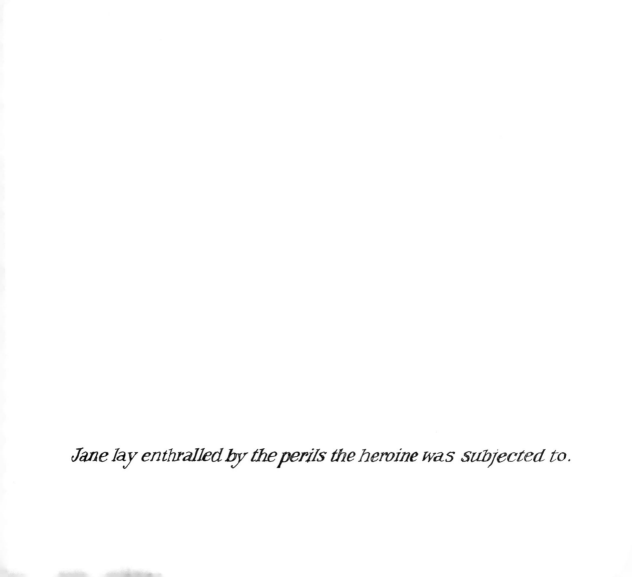

Jane lay enthralled by the perils the heroine was subjected to.

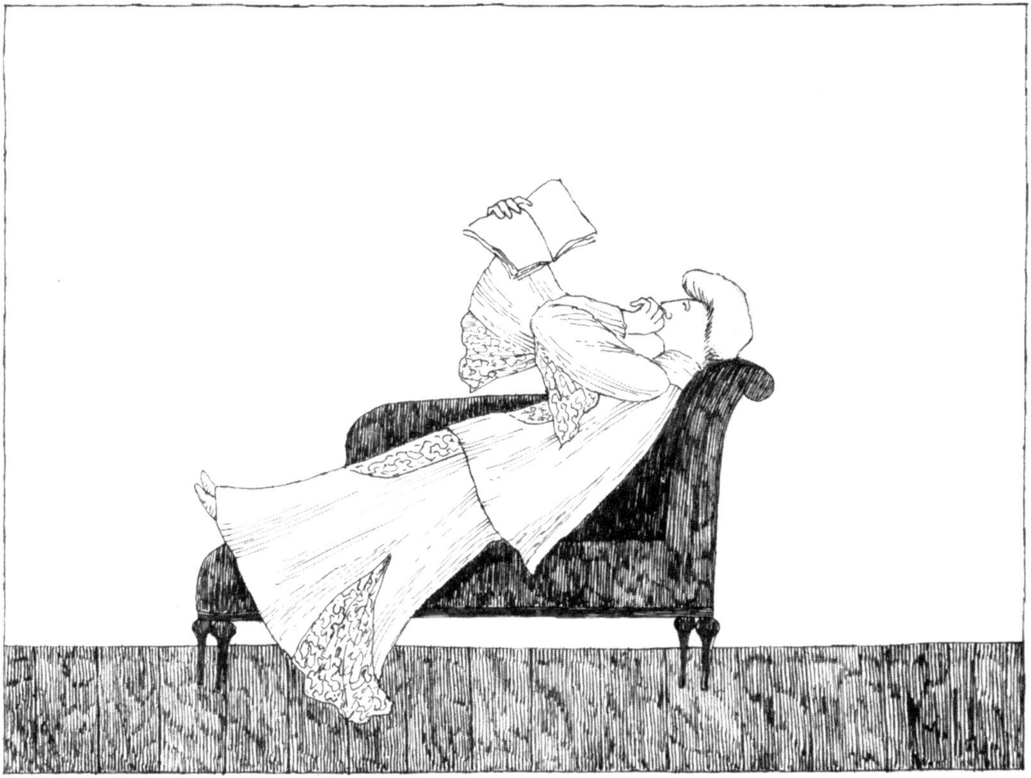

The clock struck for the first time that day; she started up from the midst of a trainwreck.

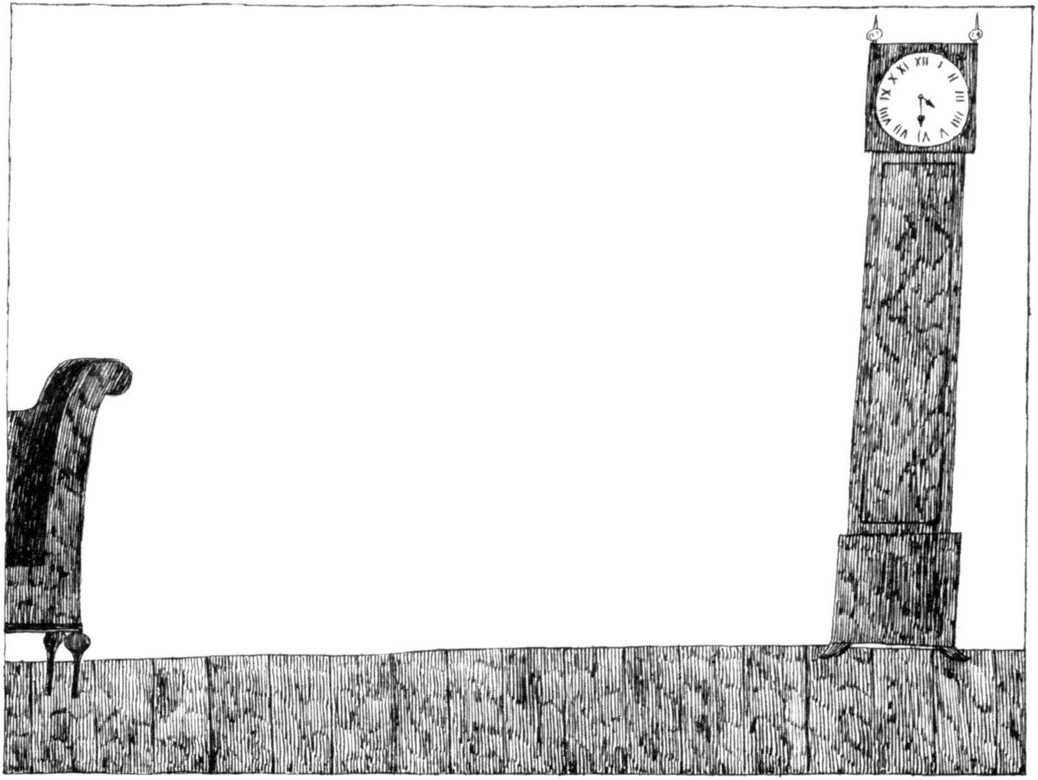

'I must go and shop for dinner' she said, drawn to the window by the curious glare.

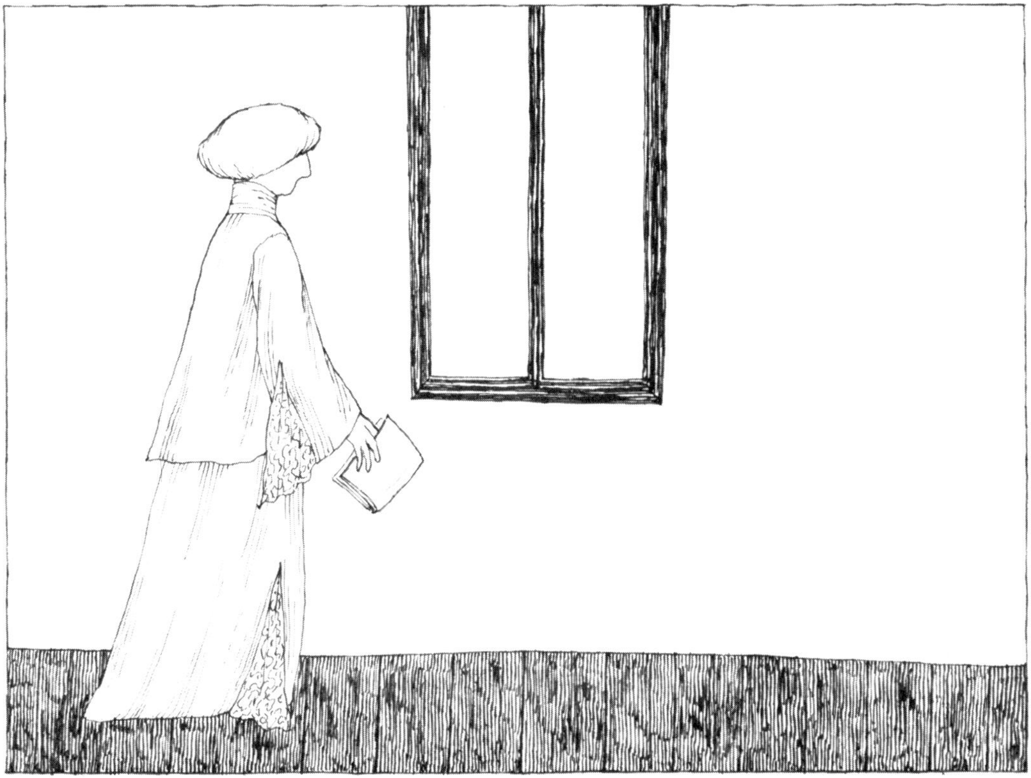

The snow was far too deep for her to go to the village.

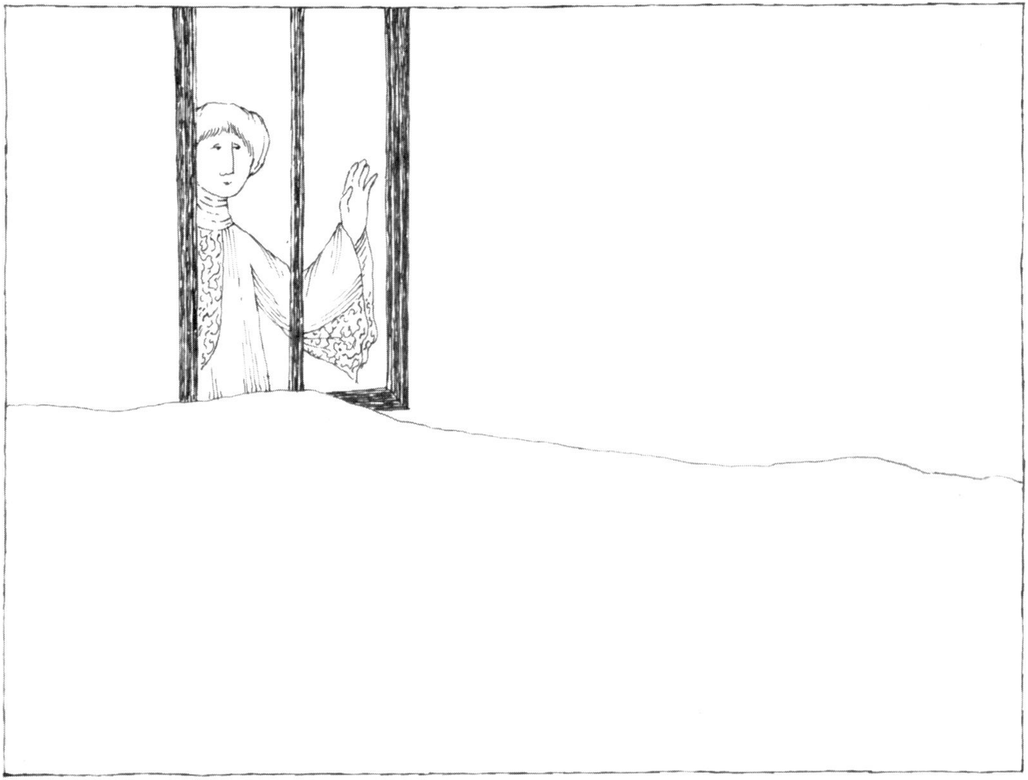

She read to the end of the novelette and then asked
herself 'What shall I do about dinner?'.

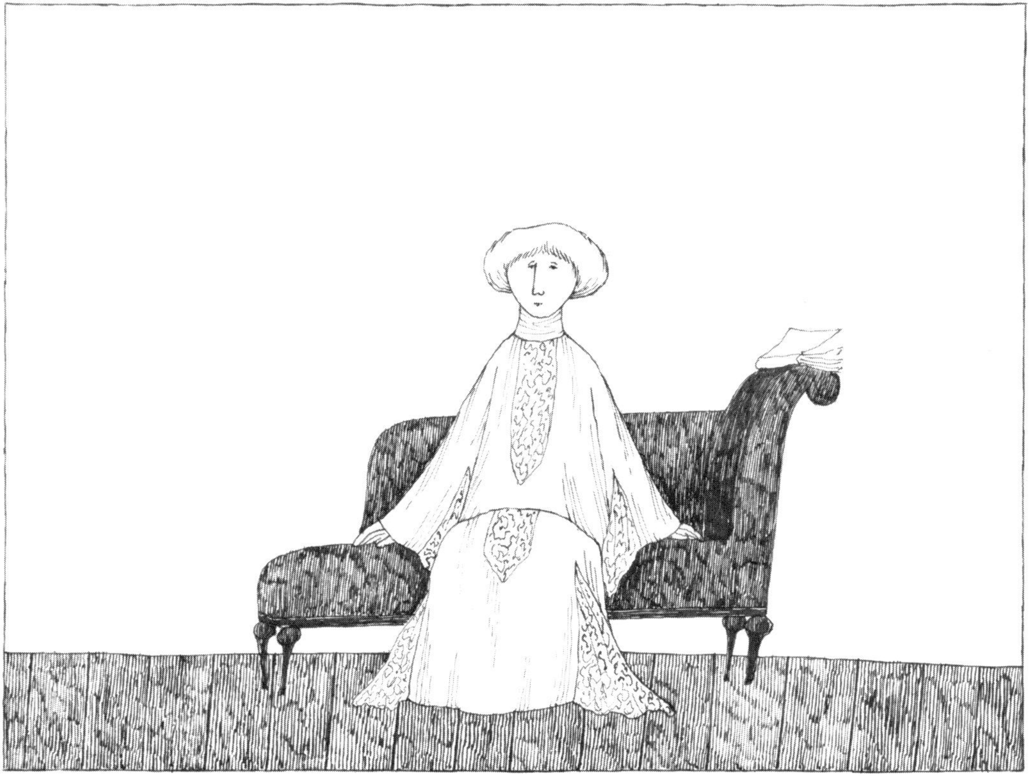

The kitchen yielded nothing but an unopened box of soda crackers in the cupboard.

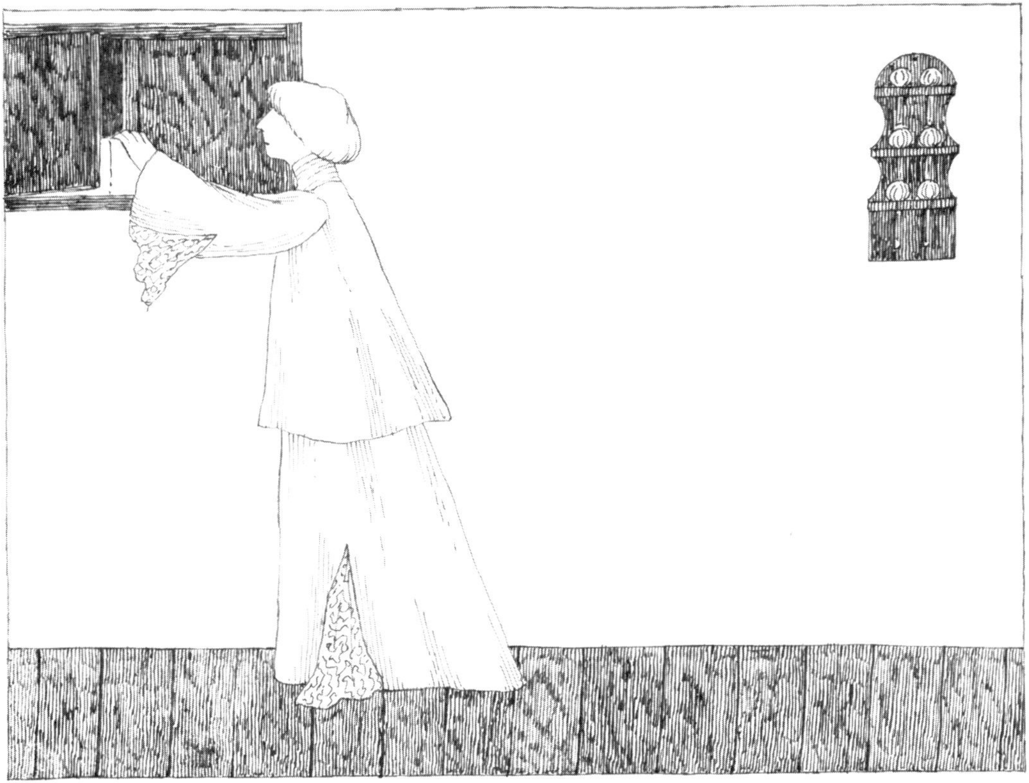

Charles came in and said 'What are we having for dinner?'.

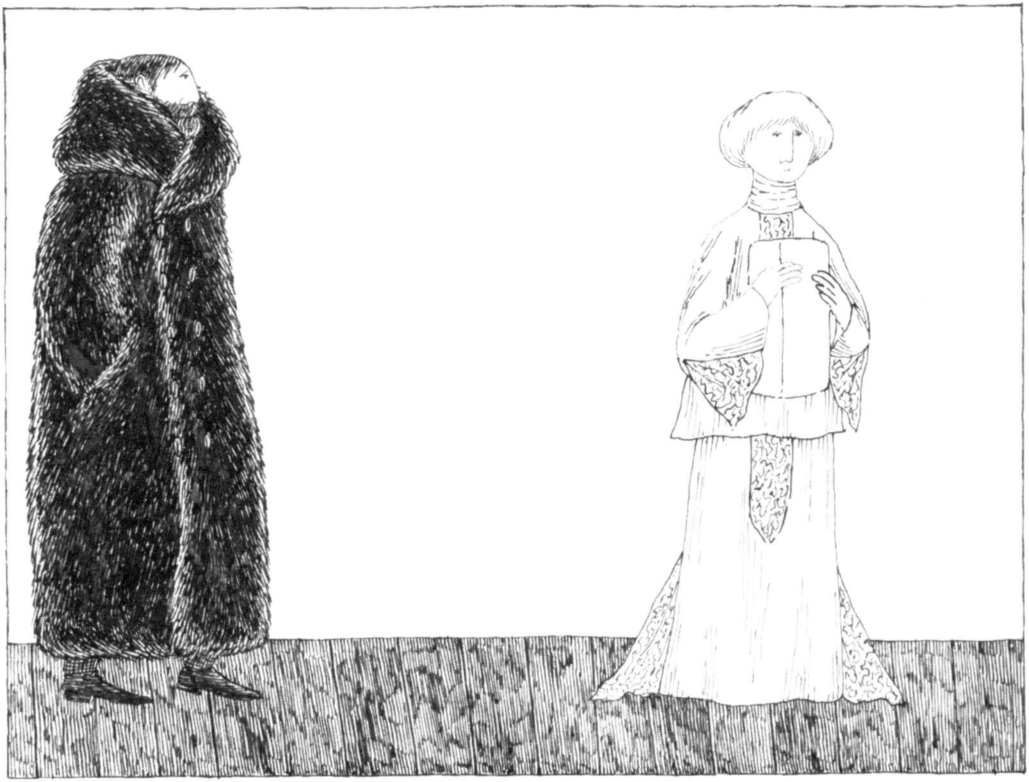

'Soda crackers,' she said 'but I'll make a delicious white sauce to go over them'.

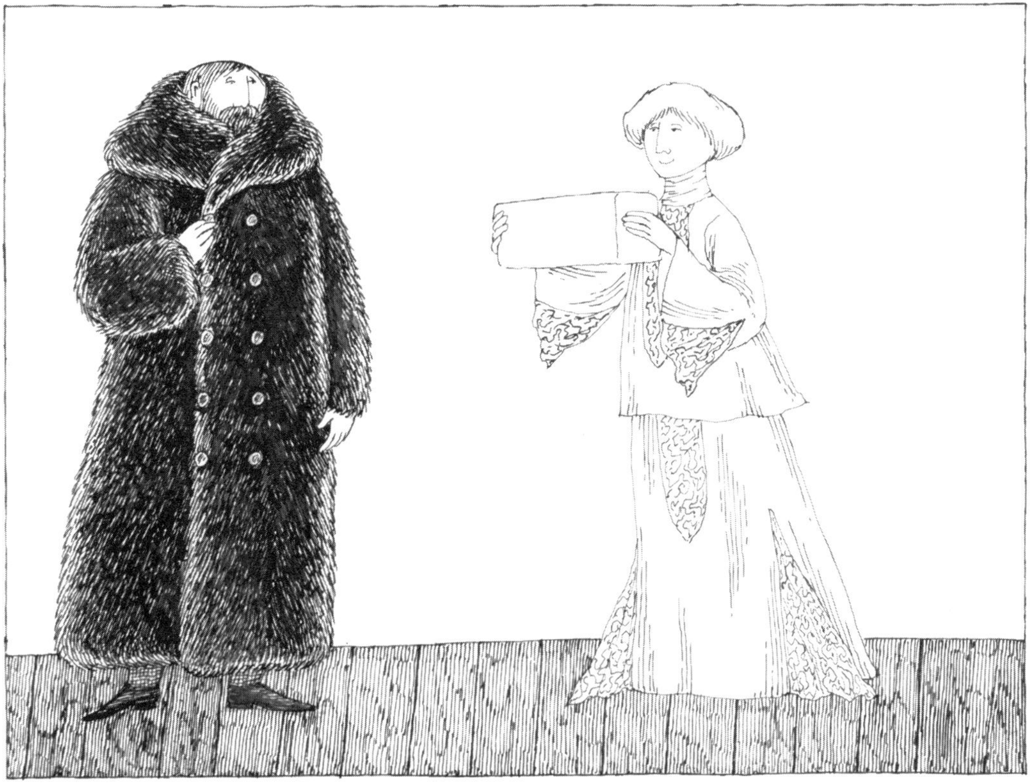

*She took flour and water, and mixed some of each
together on the stove.*

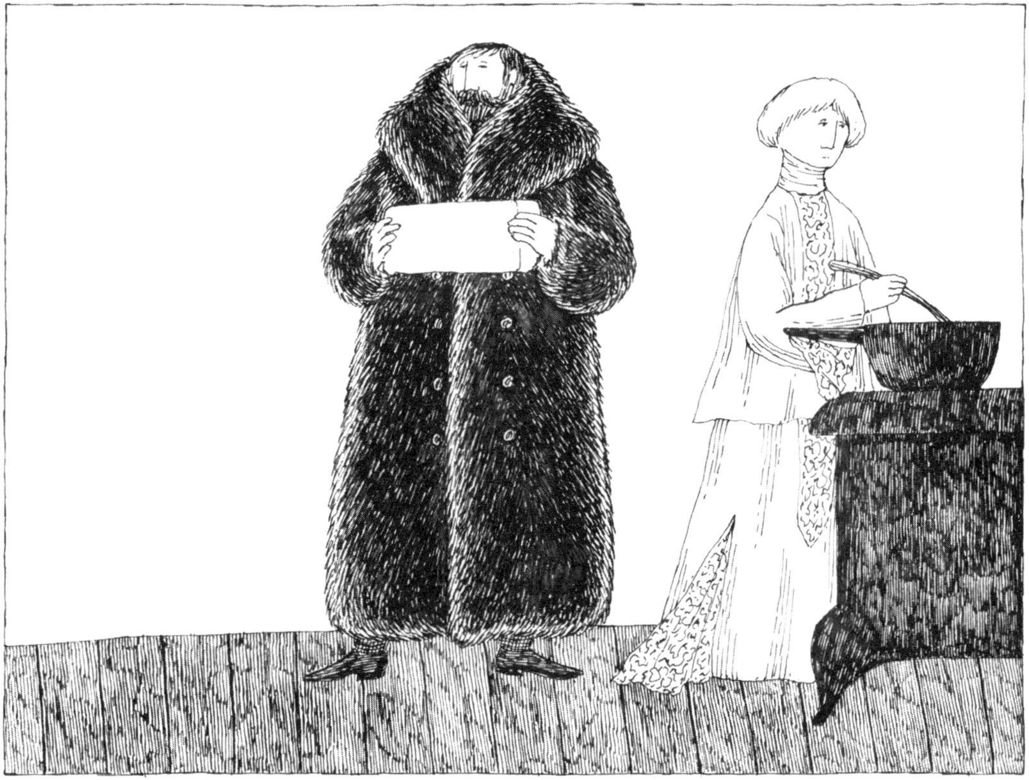

George came in, stirred the sauce about, and said 'It's too thick'.

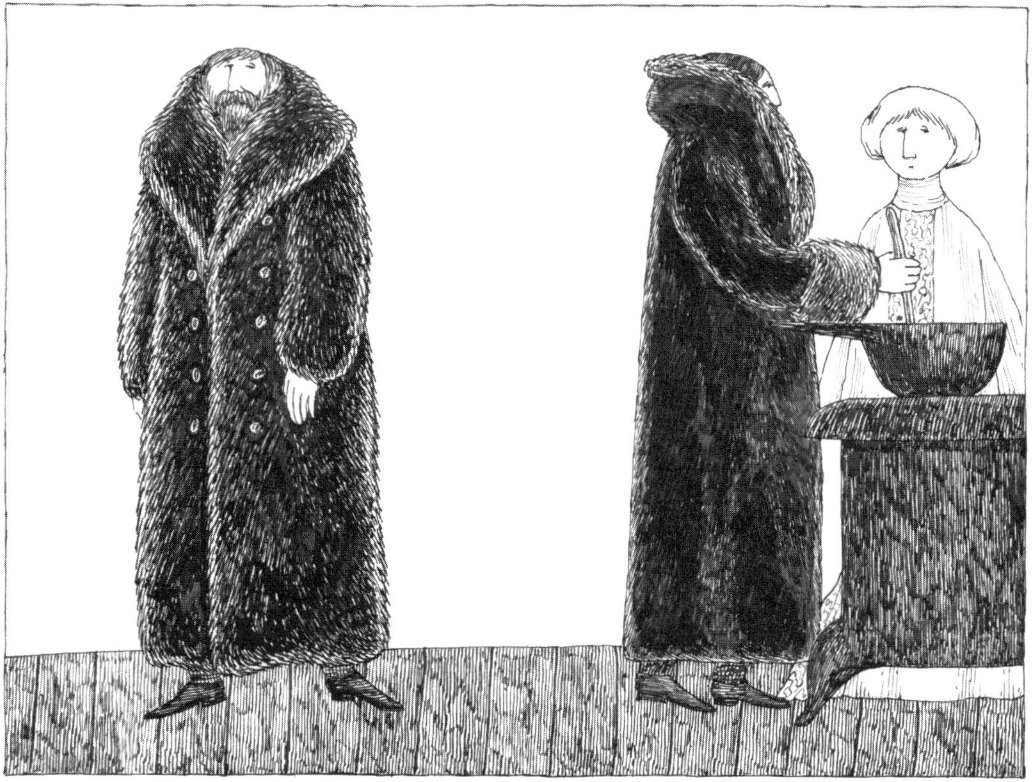

Jane added a quantity of water.

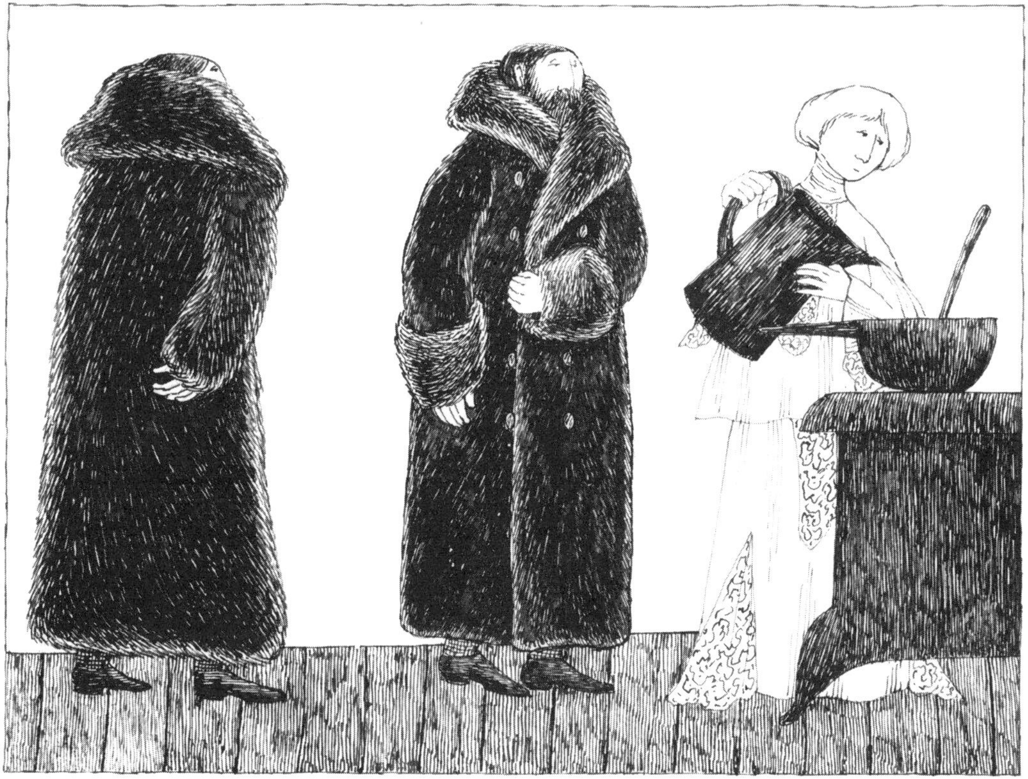

Anne came in as George was tasting it.

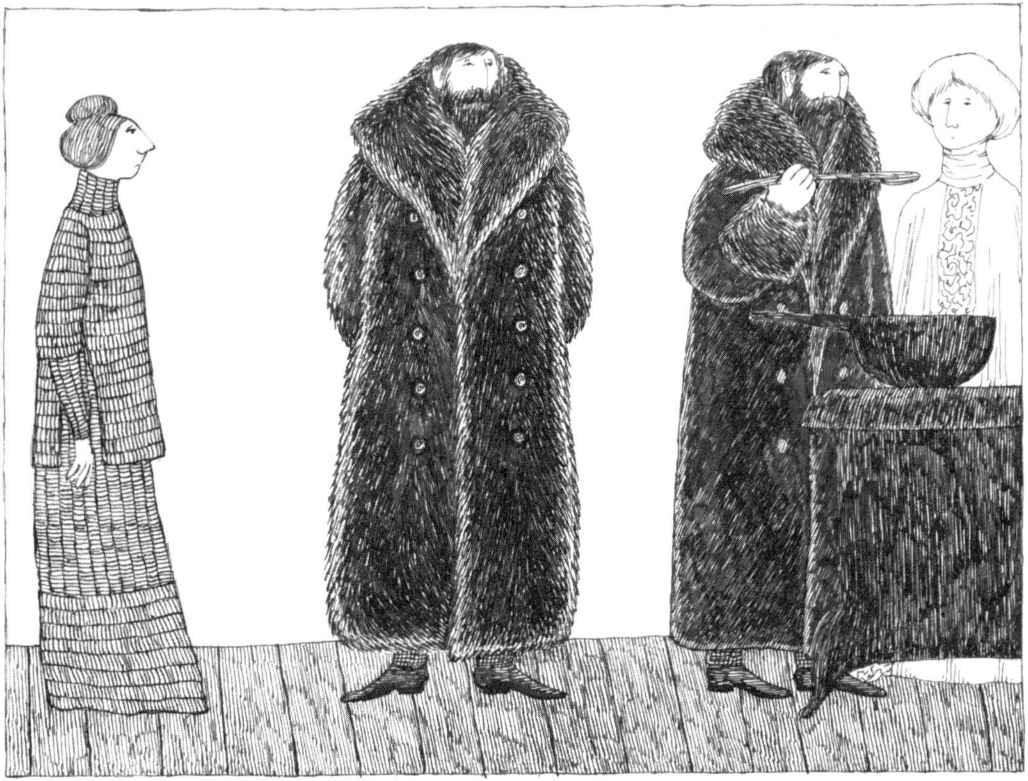

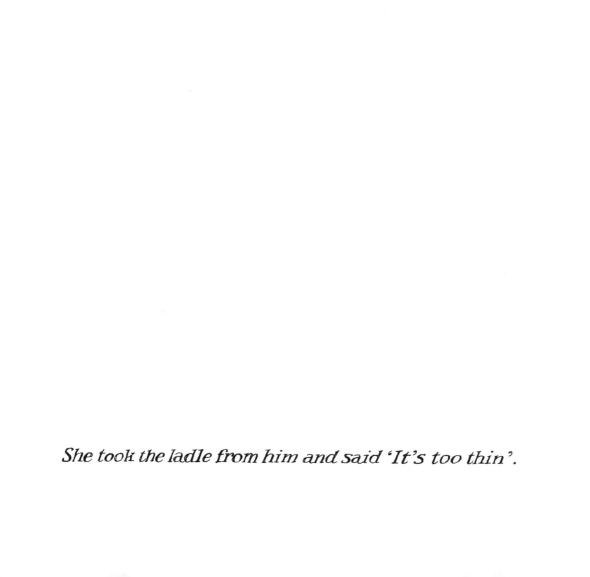

She took the ladle from him and said 'It's too thin'.

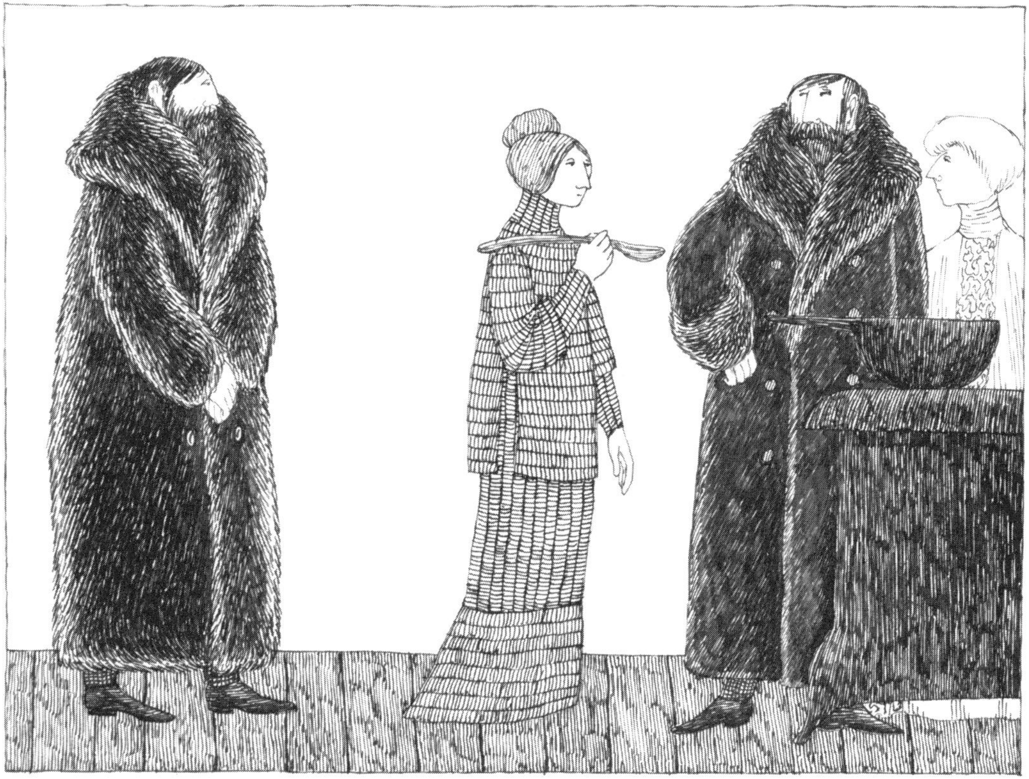

Jane added an amount of flour.

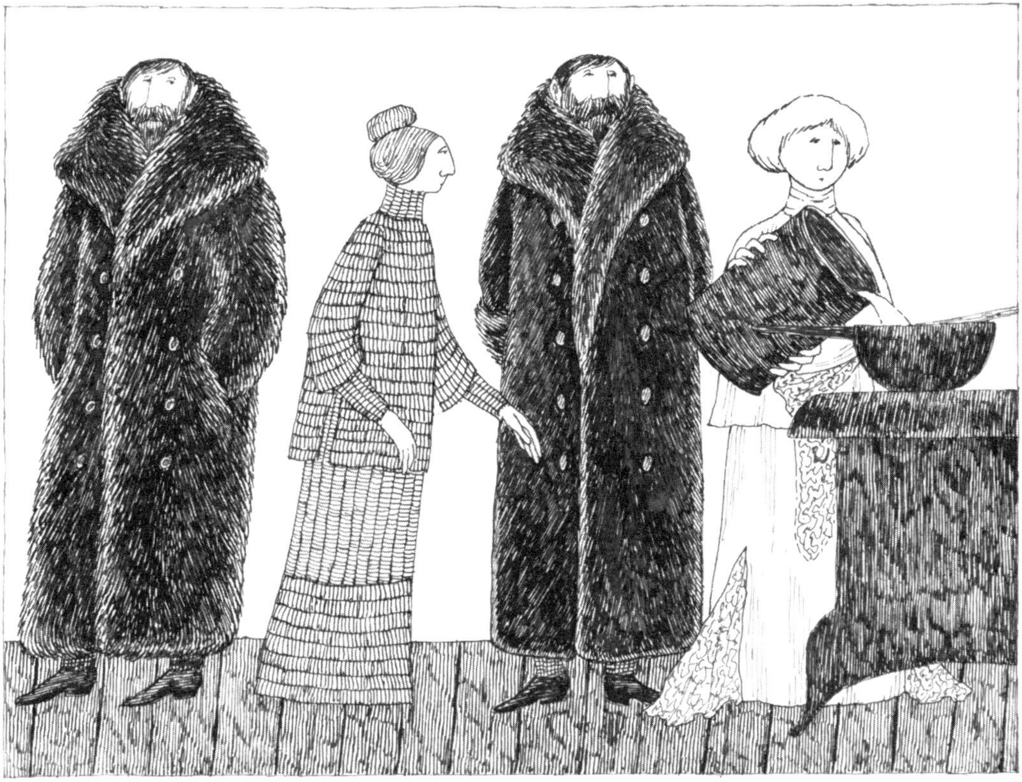

William came in as Anne was sampling it again.

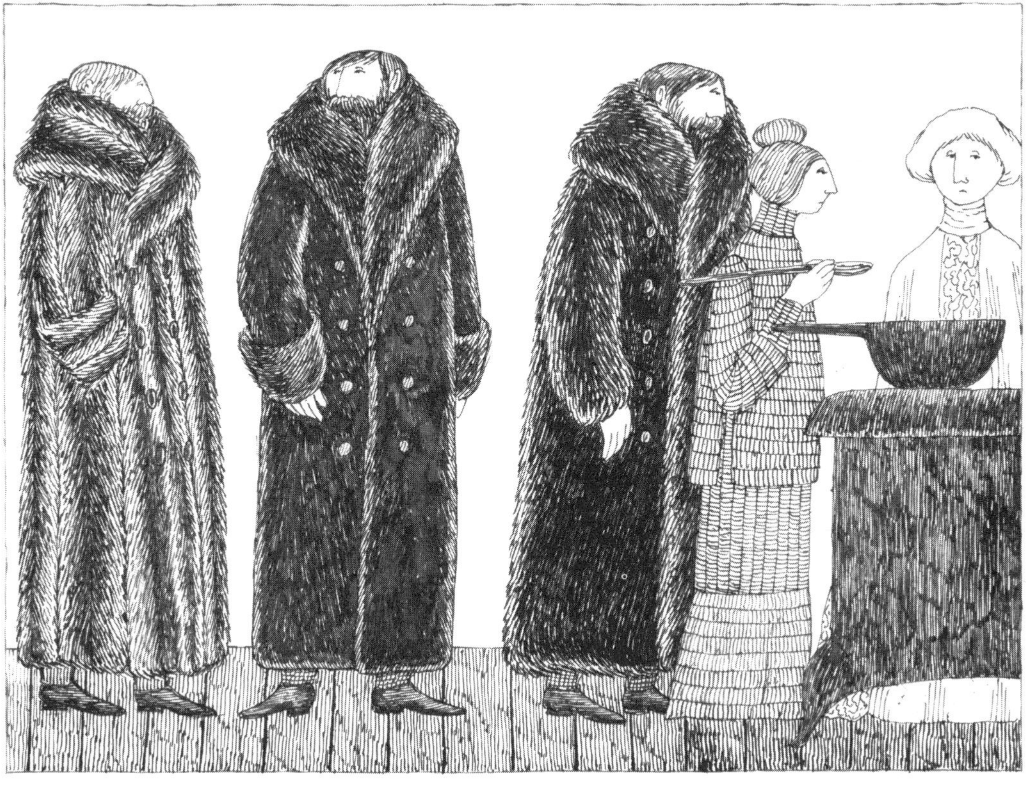

He stuck his finger in it and said 'It's lumpy'.

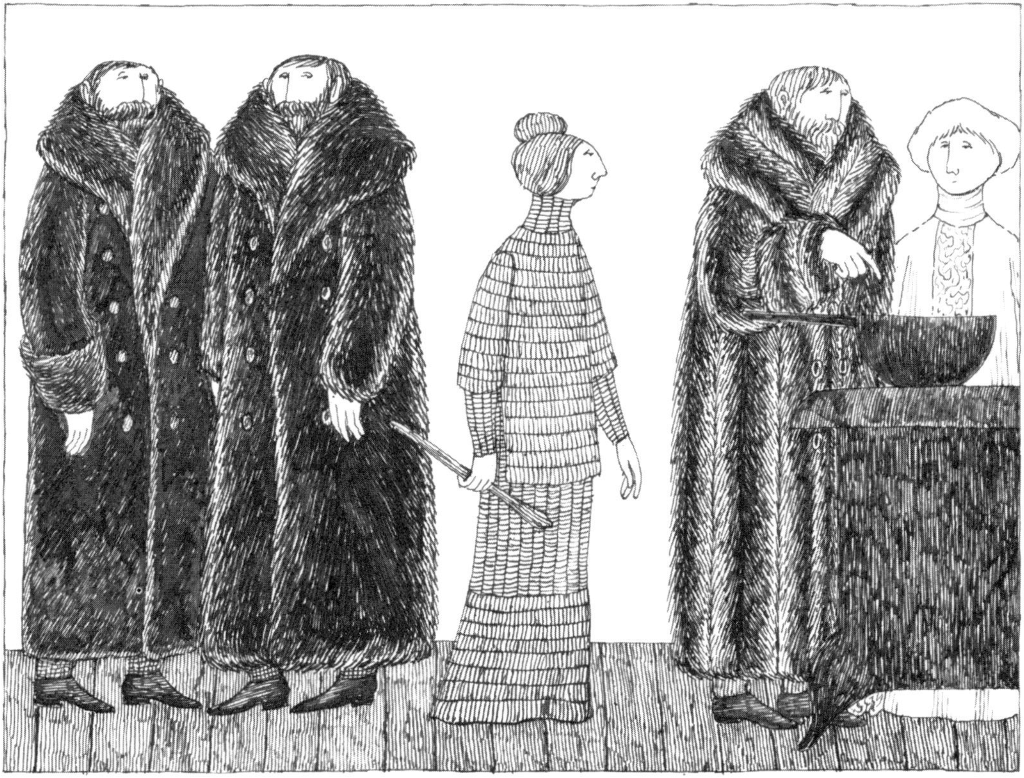

Jane poured in water to dissolve the lumps, so that it was too thin once again.

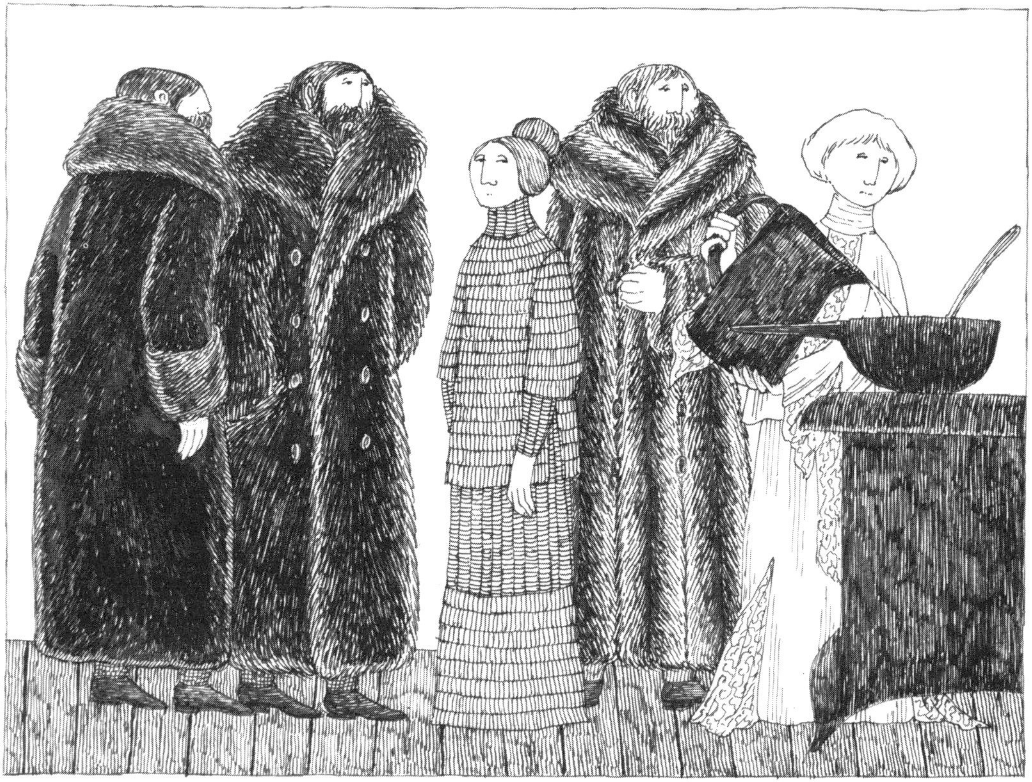

She dumped in flour, so that it became a second time too thick.

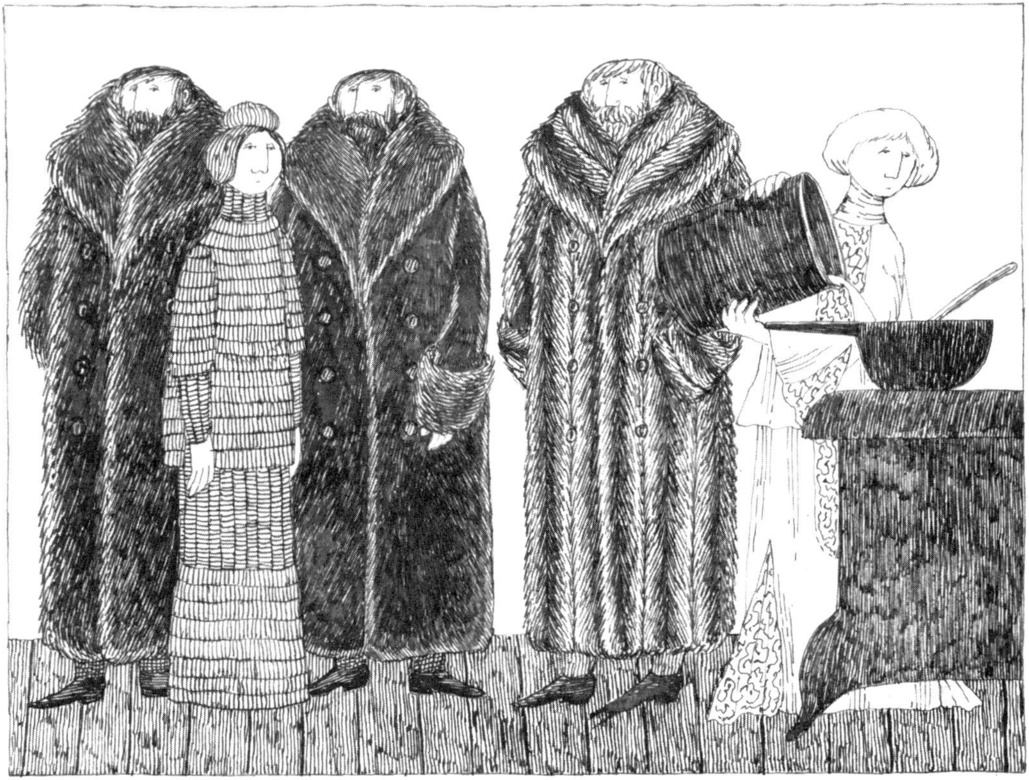

This went on until there was so much white sauce, it
filled every available receptacle.

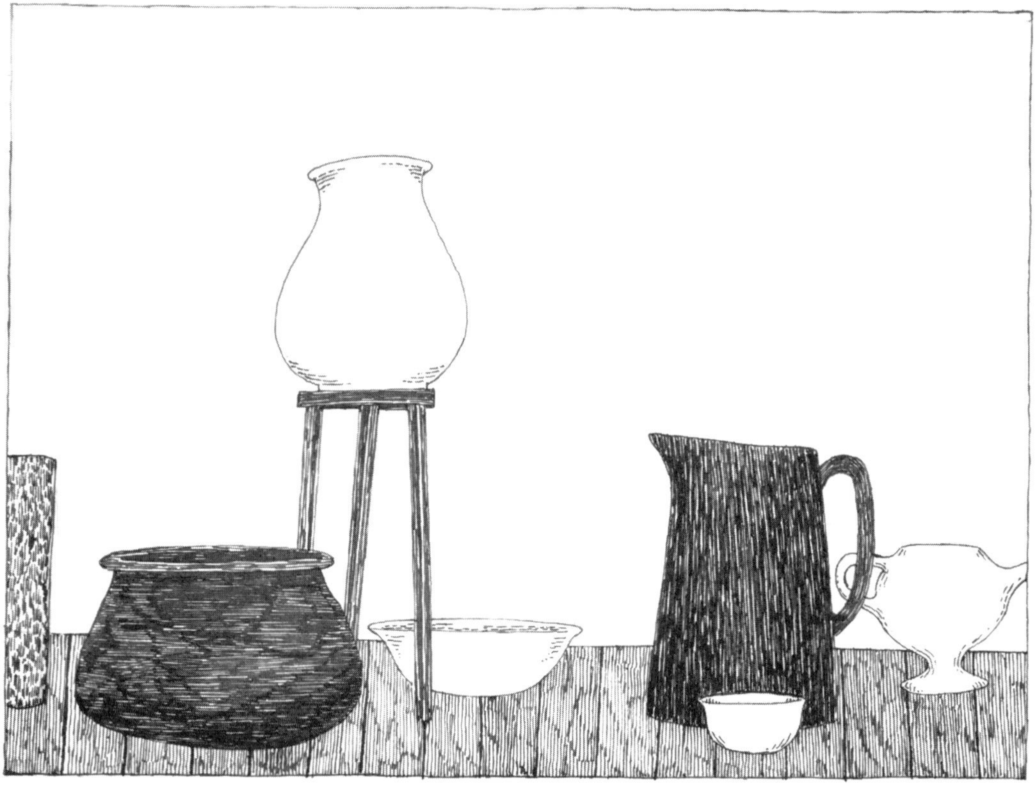

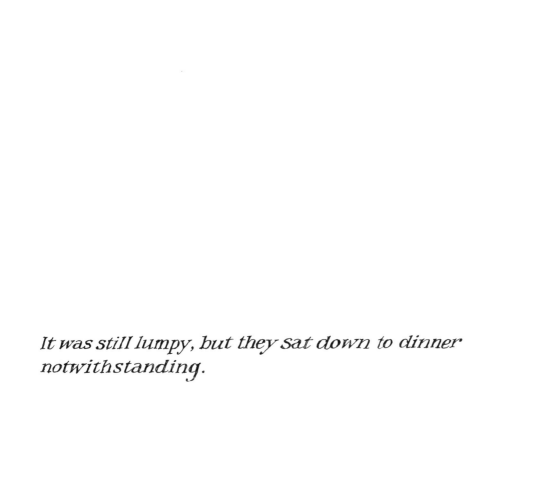

It was still lumpy, but they sat down to dinner notwithstanding.

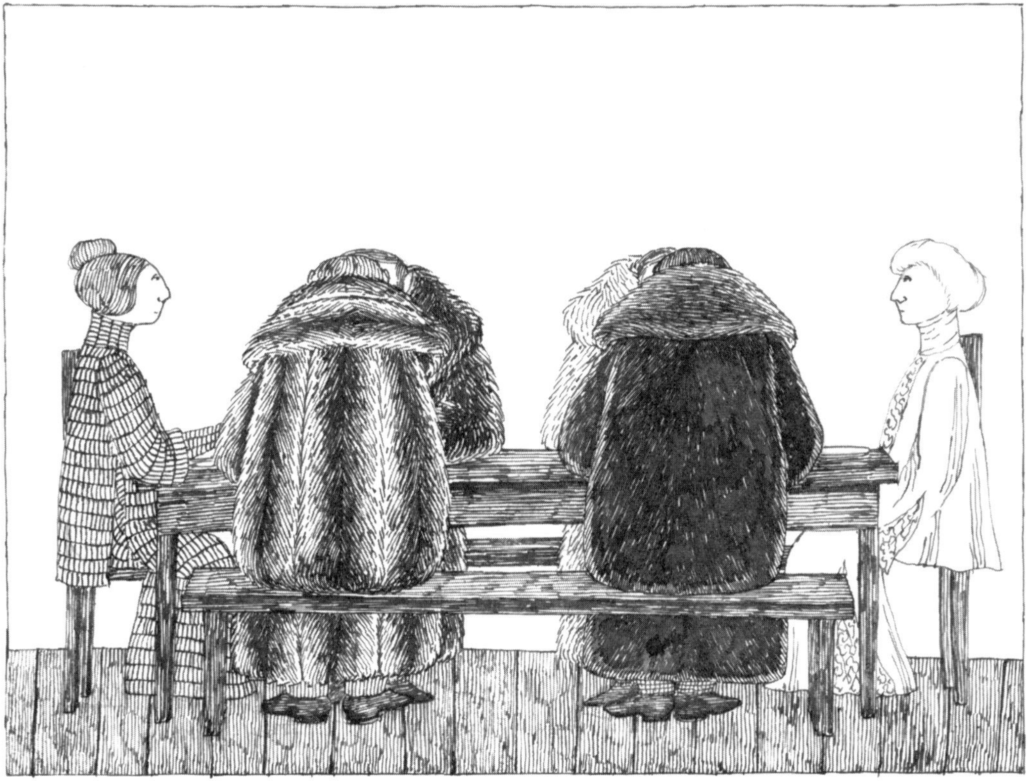

In the ensuing weeks white sauce appeared at least once, and often two or three times, at every meal, even breakfast.

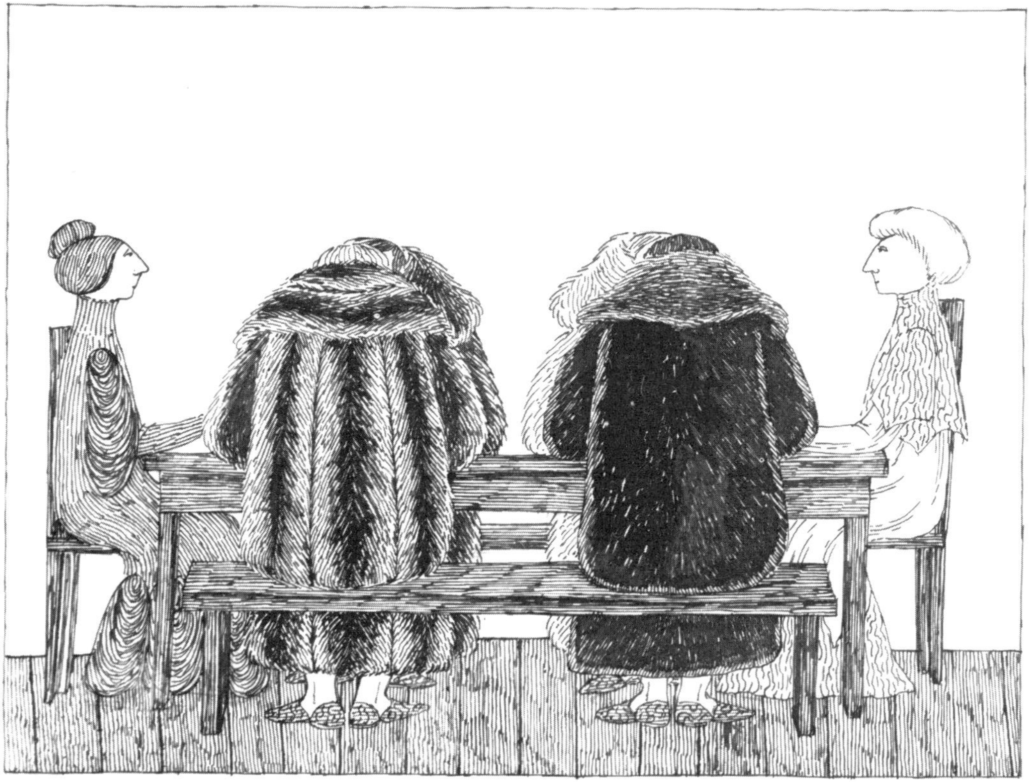

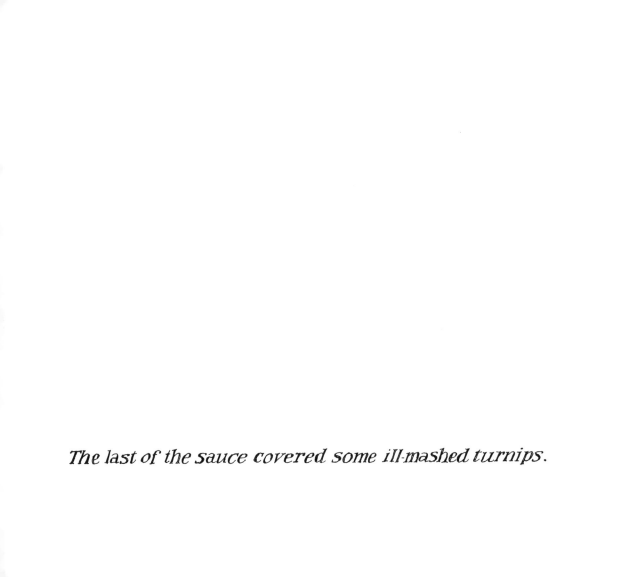

The last of the sauce covered some ill-mashed turnips.

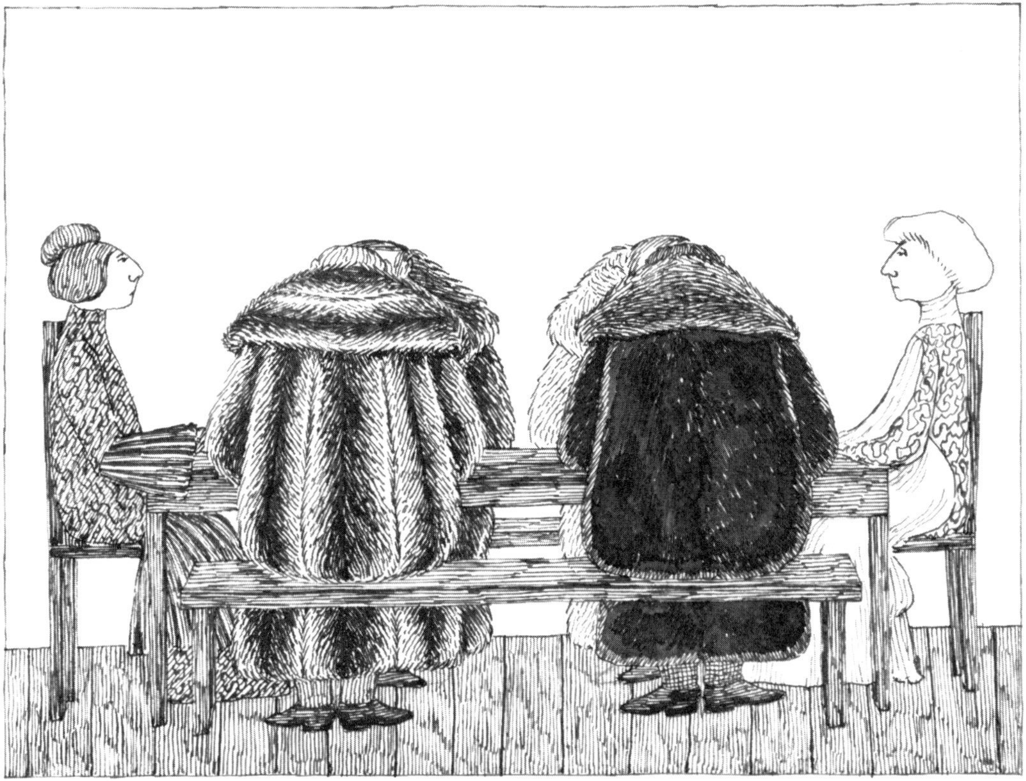

Just after the meal concluded Henry suddenly died.

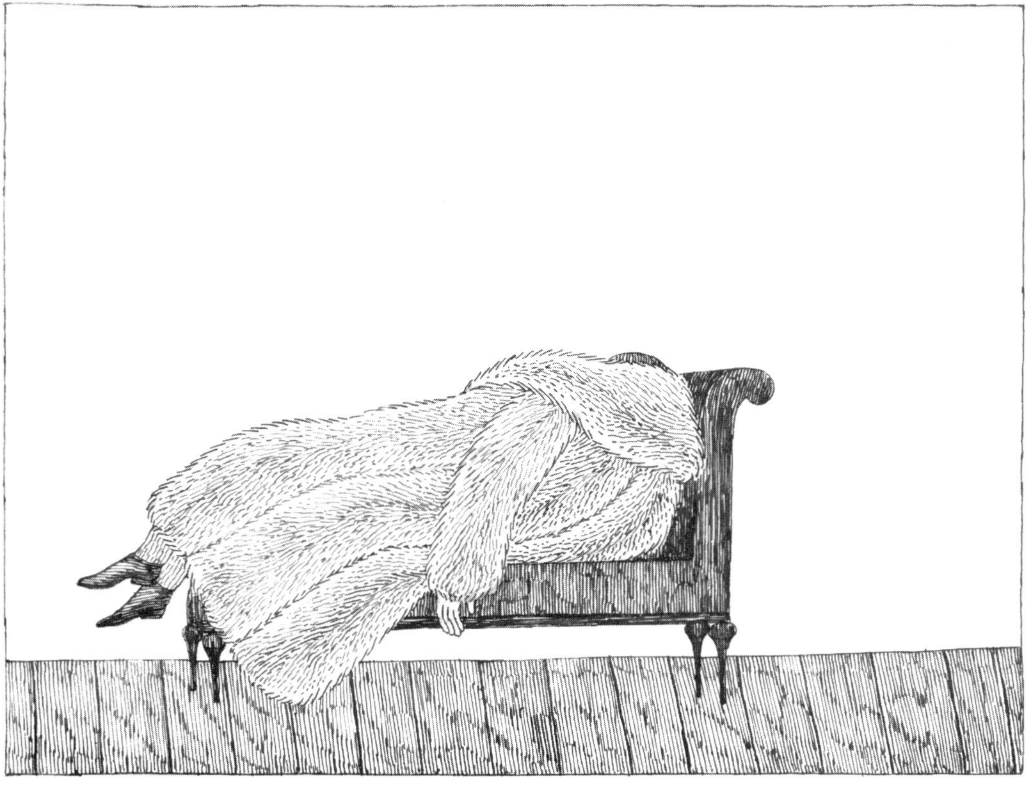

It was Christmas Eve as it happened.

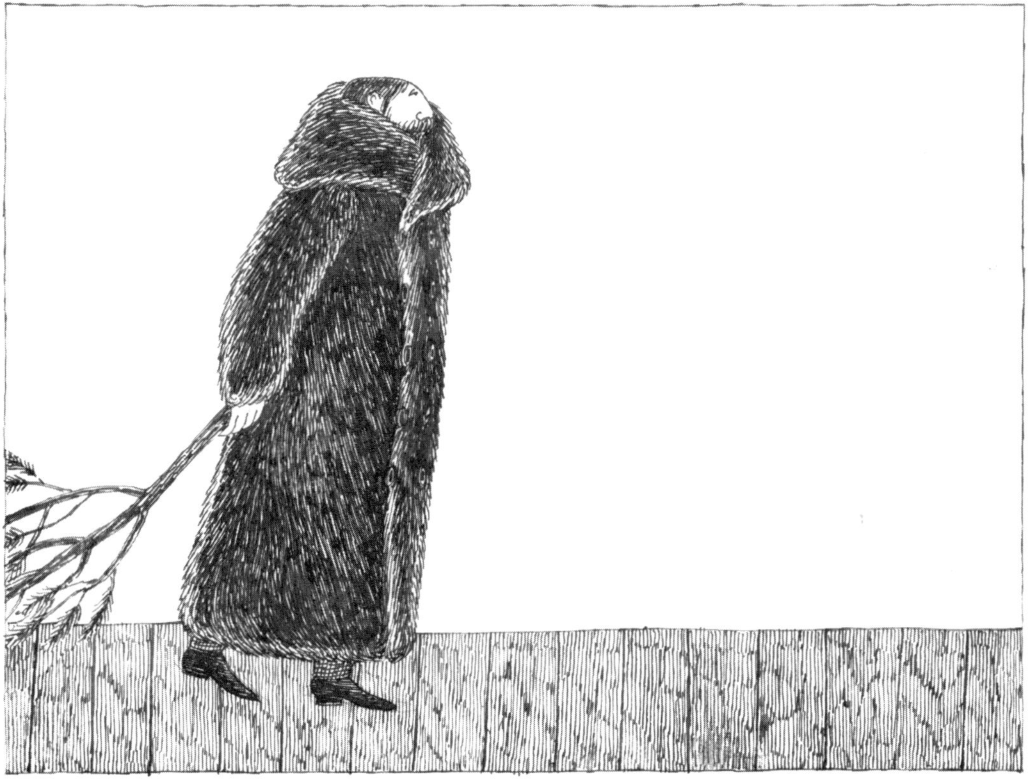

Jane, Anne, George, and William painted all the ornaments a dull black.

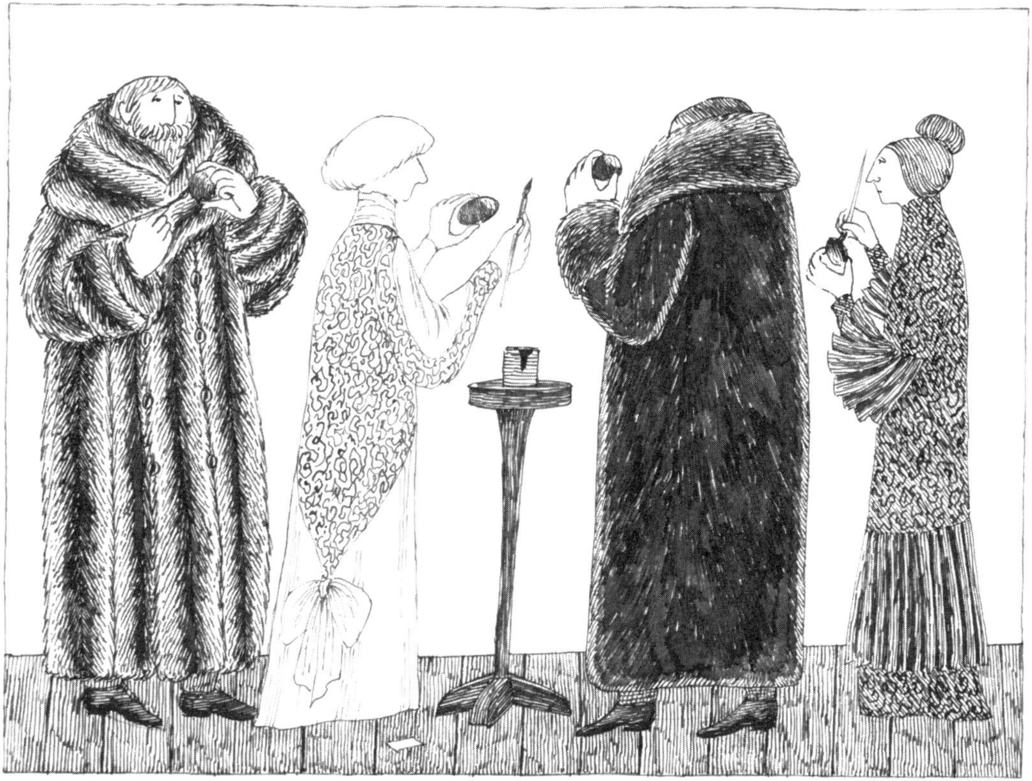

Charles went to the village for black candles.

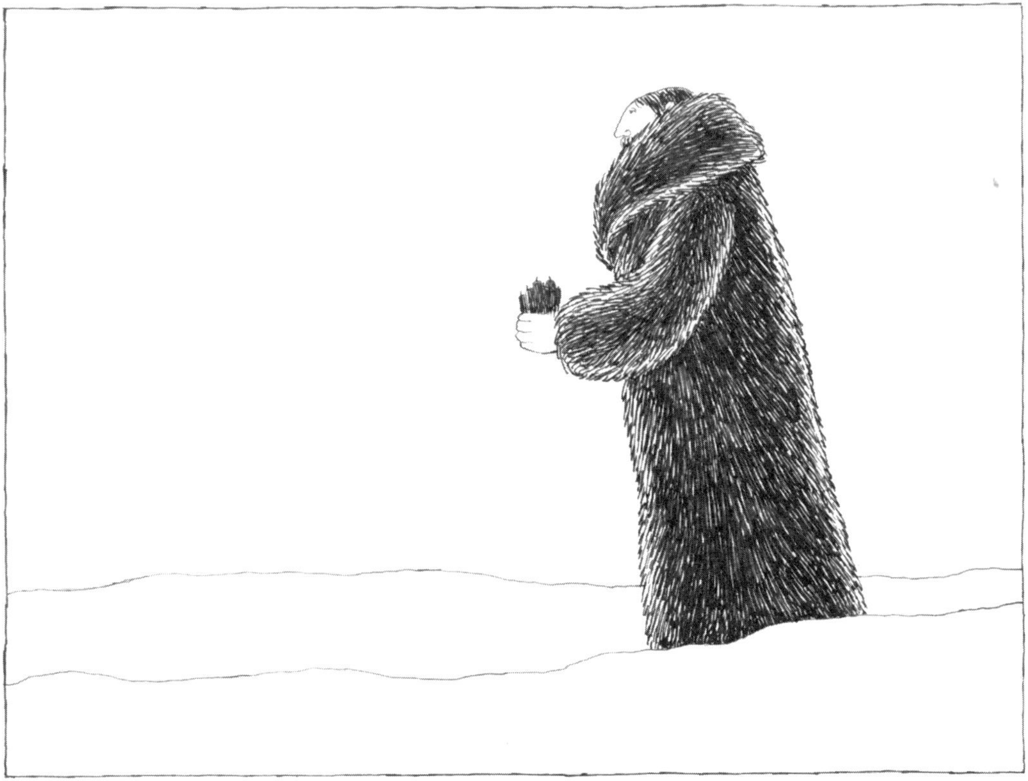

Snow was falling again as they finished trimming the tree.

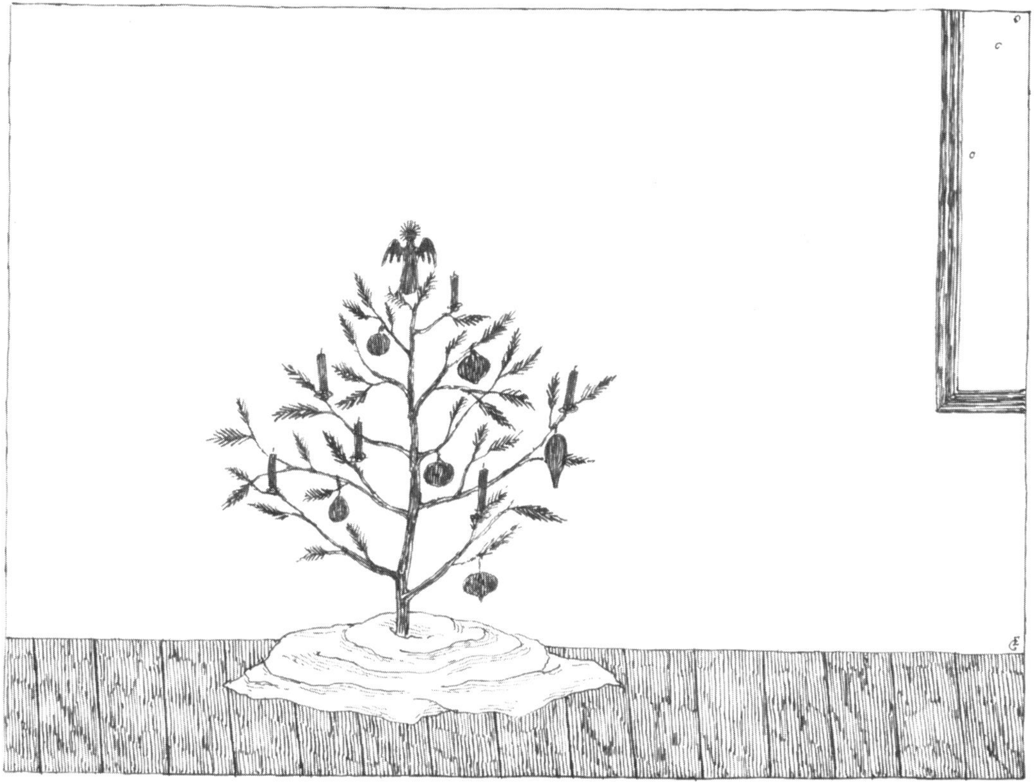

ALSO BY EDWARD GOREY *The Unstrung Harp; The Listing Attic; The Doubtful Guest; The Object-Lesson; The Bug Book; The Fatal Lozenge; The Hapless Child; The Curious Sofa; The Willowdale Handcar; The Beastly Baby; The Vinegar Works: The Gashlycrumb Tinies, The Insect God; The West Wing; The Wuggly Ump; The Nursery Frieze; The Sinking Spell; The Remembered Visit; The Pious Infant; The Evil Garden; The Inanimate Tragedy; The Gilded Bat; The Utter Zoo; The Blue Aspic; The Iron Tonic; The Osbick Bird; The Chinese Obelisks; The Epiplectic Bicycle; The Sopping Thursday; The Deranged Cousins; The Eleventh Episode; [The Untitled Book]; The Awdrey-Gore Legacy; The Lavender Leotard; The Black Doll; The Disrespectful Summons; The Abandoned Sock; The Lost Lions; The Glorious Nosebleed; L'Heure bleue; The Broken Spoke; Les Passementeries Horribles; The Loathsome Couple; The Green Beads; Les Urnes Utiles; Le Mélange Funeste; The Dwindling Party*

THE SECRETS *The Other Statue; The Night Bandage et al (in preparation)*

DRAWINGS *Leaves from a Mislaid Album; Cat^{e}gor y*

COMPILATIONS *Amphigorey; Amphigorey Too*

MISCELLANEOUS *Dracula: a Toy Theatre; Dogear Wryde Postcards: various series*

WITH PETER NEUMEYER *Donald and the ... ; Donald Has a Difficulty; Why we have day and night*

WITH VICTORIA CHESS *Fletcher and Zenobia; Fletcher and Zenobia Save the Circus*

DRAWINGS FOR *The Jumblies*, EDWARD LEAR; *The Dong with a Luminous Nose*, EDWARD LEAR; *Story for Sara*, ALPHONSE ALLAIS; *The Salt Herring*, CHARLES CROS